LIFE:

An Ellipsis

By

J.J. BHATT

ISBN:
9798757671642

Title:

LIFE:
An Ellipsis

Author:

J.J. Bhatt

Published and Distributed by Amazon and Kindle worldwide.

This book is manufactured in the Unites States of America.

Recent Books by J.J. Bhatt

(Available from Amazon/Kindle)

HUMAN ENDEAVOR: *Essence & Mission/ A Call for Global Awakening,* (2011)

ROLLING SPIRITS: *Being Becoming /*A Trilogy, (2012)

ODYSSEY OF THE DAMNED: *A Revolving Destiny,* (2013).

PARISHRAM: *Journey of the Human Spirits,* (2014).

TRIUMPH OF THE BOLD: *A Poetic Reality,* (2015).

THEATER OF WISDOM, *(2016).*

MAGNIFICENT QUEST: *Life, Death & Eternity,* (2016).

ESSENCE OF INDIA: *A Comprehensive Perspective,* (2016).

ESSENCE OF CHINA: *Challenges & Possibilities,* (2016).

BEING & MORAL PERSUASION: *A Bolt of Inspiration,* (2017).

REFELCTIONS, RECOLLECTIONS & EXPRESSIONS, (2018).

ONE, TWO, THREE... ETERNITY: *A Poetic Odyssey,* (2018).

INDIA: *Journey of Enlightenment,* (2019a).

SPINNING MIND, SPINNING TIME: *C'est la vie,* (2019b).Book 1.

MEDITATION ON HOLY TRINITY, *(2019c), Book 2.*

ENLIGHTENMENT: *Fiat lux,* (2019d), Book 3.

BEING IN THE CONTEXTUAL ORBIT: *Rhythm, Melody & Meaning, (2019e).*

QUINTESSENCE: *Thought & Action,* (2019f).

THE WILL TO ASCENT: *Power of Boldness & Genius,* (2019g).

RIDE ON A SPINNING WHEEL: *Existence Introspected, (2020a).*

A FLASH OF LIGHT: *Splendors, Perplexities & Riddles, (2020b).*

ON A ZIG ZAG TRAIL: *The Flow of Life*, (2020c).

UNBOUNDED: *An Inner Sense of Destiny* (2020d).

REVERBERATIONS: The *Cosmic Pulse, (2020e).*

LIGHT & DARK: *Dialogue and Meaning,* (2021a).

ROLLING REALITY: *Being in flux, (2021b).*

FORMAL SPLENDOR: *The Inner Rigor,* (2021c).

TEMPORAL TO ETERNAL: *Unknown Expedition,* (2021d).

TRAILBLAZERS: *Spears of Courage*, (2021e).

TRIALS & ERRORS: *A Path to Human Understanding*, (2021f).

MEASURE OF HUMAN EXPERIENCE: *Brief Notes,* (2021g).

BEING BECOMING, (2022a)

INVINCIBLE,(2022b).

VALIDATION: *The Inner Realm of Essence*, (2022c).

LET'S ROLL: *Brave Hearts,* (2022d).

LIFE: *An Ellipsis, (2022e).*

THE CODE: *Destiny* (2022f).

Preface

LIFE: *An Ellipsis* **is our existence what is essentially an ever expanding dotted sphere of possibilities. That is the fascinating challenge yet to be fulfilled within the framework of a given finite time.**

In its big picture, life remains an apodictic reality inevitably rolling toward the "Noble Death." Who knows beyond death whether we are still the eternal consciousness able to inspire the young minds? That is why it is paramount, what we do while being alive matters the most.

J.J. Bhatt

5

Contents

7

Being
As Is

And from the
Flow of thoughts
I dare
Look far through
Eternity
Where beauty of
My truth waits
To be experienced

Alas,
Death seems
Only bump on
The way to such
A fascinating
Anticipation to be
Fulfilled

Let it be
Meaning of
The journey
From here to
Over there that
I alone must know...

Weak links

Sometimes
It's a
"Mystery"
That keeps me
Dancing the
Whole night, but

Not
Opening the
Final curtain and
I ask, "Why?"

Sometimes
I call it
"Peace"
But keeps me
Struggling for
A long and
I ask, "Why?"

Sometimes
I am lost and
Spins into the
Constant chaos
And confusion,
And don't know,
"Why?"

Truth!

In pure
Abstraction,
What if nothing
Exists but the
Shallow opinions
Of the finite humans

In the
World of constant
Struggles, what if
Nothing matters, but
Ephemeral dreams;
Keeps vanishing
Through the time

In the
World of greed
What if nothing
Exists but the
Corrupted human
Spirit lacking any
Distant vision...

Fortitude

Imagination
What a greatest
Gift of human
Creativity

It's
The projection
Of infinite ideas
Beaming through
The core of any
Unknown

Odyssey
Of the intelligent
Mind
What an eternal
Mélange of mysteries,
Magic's and madness

And yet,
He keeps
Walking with
Fortitude and
Deep commitment...

Anomaly

And the
Kabuki dance
Keeps going among
Zillion realities
All over in every
Universe

That is a
Tough-of-war
Between creation,
Sustenance, destruction
And back again offering
In return nothing but
Paradoxes, contradictions
And riddles

Meanwhile
Human mind
Seemed caught into
This eternal anomaly:
From Impermanence
To the permanence and
Unable to think beyond...

Quintessence

What is this
Weird notion
Called,
"Durable Peace"
And why is it
Not well honored
By the half-evolved,
Human still

What is
This paradox
Called, "Thinking
Human" who's
Not yet ready to
Discover his truth

Why is he still
Ignorant in the
Age of so much
Info; not knowing,
"Where is his real
Destiny"

Steady,
Not Yet

**Being is
Packed with
Beliefs either
Rational or
Irrational**

**Being is
Either on a
Right track or
Otherwise**

**That's his
Essence driving
The existence
Forward but
Never a steady
Experience...**

Fingerprints

From,
"A Space Odyssey"
We saw for the
First time,
HAL,
Then thinking
Robot could replace
Intelligent beings

Today,
It's a reality
For million others
Like it are already
In-making today

Don't
Be surprised
Soon they would
Call the shots in
Many walks of life

Are we
Seeing the
Fingerprints of
Human future either
Good or what?

Being & Identity

Human
Identity what
An issue of many
Debates

Is it his
Inner spirit
We're
Questioning
Is it his
Mental machine
In doubt already

Is human
A finite soul
With a locked-in
Birth, life and death
Only or

Is he still the
Intelligent
Continuum of the
Eternally spinning
Wheel may be!

Delinquents

It's in this
Very dynamic
Reality
We're jumping
Back and forth
Between

Prescriptive
And descriptive,
Between absolute
And relative or
Whatever we
Think of

It's a very
Murky world
We're breathing
Through every
Night and day,
Right and wrong ,
Good or not and
Meanwhile we're
Stuck on the road
To the enlightenment...

Fading
Light!

**Blind
Obedience is
A blatant insult
To the dignity of
Any intelligent
Being**

**I mean,
Into this
Techno-spinning
Big wheel**

**Where kids
Soon learn,
"What to accept
And what to be
Deleted with
A simple click"**

**May be
There's no
Room for judgment
When they're being
Driven by the luring
Smart machines...**

Life
Cycle

**Still the
Sphere of
Darkness
Overwhelms
His experience**

**Why let
Time slip away
Without knowing
The very meaning
Of the Self**

**Let him
Evolve out
His ignorance
Let him
Be free and
Happy again**

Fire within

We' would
Be kissing in
The heaven of
Our dreams,
Today

If I had
Just listened to
The whispers of
Your heart

We would be
Dancing in the
Realm of love,
Forever

If I had I
Listened to
Your sweet song
Carrying deep meaning...

Conceptual Being

Who
Knows?
Truth
May be
Nothing but
The mental
Processing of
Abstraction or
Something more

We
Can't ignore
Mystiques,
Creative artists
And billion others
Who too are after
The same eternal
Riddle called,
"Truth"

Clarion
Bells

It's a little
Inconvenience,
While
Rolling through
The fields of grief
And despair

If we
Remain
A collective force
Steady on the right
Track,

Of course
We would be
A dynamic flow of
Wishes, dreams
And a noble mission

Let us
Roar with full joy,
"Humanity above all"
"Humanity above all"
"Humanity
Above all forever..."

Third Eye

I struggle,
Therefore 'am
An ordinary
Being and

Looking for
A right place
Through the
Third Eye

That's why
I must
Value my
Brief existence
Before it's too late

Let I be
A freewill so
I can reciprocate
My responsibility
In my time...

Measure

Being
Seeking to
Fulfill his big
Dream every time

Being
Always a rebel
To dismantle the
Old taboos and
The asinne tribal
Claims

Being
Always an
Indefatigable will
On the way to
Know his truth

Being
What a historic
Force of blunders
And million sins...

Inner
Mind

Where
An endless
Stream of
Thoughts
Keep flowing
Like the
Ripples heading
Toward the
Blue sea and to
That we call,
"Consciousness"

Consciousness
Emanating
From the
Finite beings and
Rushing toward
Infinite possibilities
And to that we call,
"Emergence, indeed."

Empty
Theater

**What's the
Him being either
Transcendental
Or Immanent
So long human
Nature doesn't
Change at the core**

**What's the
Point of the
Great One
When human is
Unable to free
Himself from the
Seven sin**

**What's the
Meaning in
Sticking to
Contradictions
When believers
Already left the
Theater while ago...**

Equal
We're

Equality is
All about having
The same social
And economic opps
For an upward
Mobility

Equality
Is to have the
Same political
And legal rights
To be fully human
Over and again

"Equality
Also must mean
Freedom tied-up
With personal
Responsibility,
Always..."

Introspection

Is it the
Failure of our
Moral strength
That is the
Consequence of
Our shaky world
Today!

Is it the
Illusion of our
Hubris
That is the
Cause of our
Constant frictions,
Today?

Is it not
The time to be
Cooperative and
Be wise, today!

Beware

Pompous
Dictators
Of today
Flexing their
Macho muscles
Every day

All busy
Projecting
Their mighty
Strength and
Exaggerating
Image to be
In charge

Crazy tyrants,
Cyber hacks and
Emerging threats
Of the nukes and
Climate change;
Bleeding humanity
In the whirlpool of
Constant insecurity
And fear...

Soul
Talking

As I
Look at you
Through the
Mirror of my
Soul

I wonder,
Is this the
Magic of love is
Real or what

As you
Look at me
Through the
Inner feelings,
Hope you're
Reckoning the
Same too

If it is
The case then
We know,
"We're
Not a dream but
A reality of our
Truth driving
Our love forever..."

Let's
Fly Away

Let me
Hold you in
My arms
And let
Your dream
Come true

Yes dear
The journeys
Just begun and
Million miles
To go

Let me
Take you
To the world
Where lovers
Sing and dance
Night and day

Come. Let's
Fly away
Where we're the
Unbroken thread of
Love all the way
Called, "Forever..."

Joy of
Life

**In the
Reflective
Pool of our
Aesthetic
Quest**

**Let us
Explore,
"How life be
The necessary
Judgment with
Moral inspiration"**

**Life
What a
Creative truth
Life
What a way
To be the
Enlightened Soul**

**Let life
Be the aesthetic
Attitude too!**

In Our Time

It's been a
Long journey
With many
Contradictions;
Waning the trust
In beliefs, in
Morality and even
Faith in humanity

It's been
Also a
Long historic
Experience, where
Death of million
Dreams have turned
Into ashes

And still
Negative forces
Keep knocking
The headlines,
Day after day!

Our Time

Our time
Seeks to be free
From the chains of
All "isms" either
Religious or whatever
Else

Our time
Seeks to be peaceful
For a very long
So the children shall
Feel safe and happy
For sure

Our time
Seeks to clean-up
The mess and be
Pals and not foes
For we
Want progress
And unity to last

Oh yes,
Our time seeks
To be good humans
To be forever...

Blowing
Winds

All creative
Endeavors begin
From a given premise
To know the truth

To a scientist,
It's the nature to
Be probed with
Reason and
To a mystique,
Its contemplation,
Indeed

To artists
Who're the
Freewill's
With no limit to
Be worried about

Alas in the end,
There is no central
Claim to this ever
Challenging game of
Truth...

My
Lady

My lady
Draws pleasure
From singing
The song of
Love always

She
Doesn't care
If folks says,
"Either positive
Or otherwise"

She's sort of
Stoic in many
Ways yet she's
The owner of
Endless feelings

That's the
Truth of
My dear lady
And I do take
Note of it, always...

Footprints

We
Two happy
Hearts flowed
Through the
Broad Boulevard
Of Barcelona in the
Year 1999

It was as if
We're the
Ripples that
Kept going through
The sea of humanity

I mean,
On that famous
Broad Boulevard of
Barcelona as
One best memory

What
Beautiful footprints
We left behind on that
Broad Boulevard
Of Barcelona in the
Year 1999...

Cool
Breeze

Life
What an
Unpredictable
Breeze at times;
Soft and so fresh

At that point,
The world
Breathes with
A clear vision

Whispering
Breeze, what a
Deep silence
To be in the
Lapse of Peace

Oh the
Refreshing
Breeze keeps the
Future hopeful to
The young braves..."

Sun Rise

Have we ever
Thought,
"Compassion is a
Necessary condition
For our harmony
And hope?"

Have we ever
Considered,
"Humanity can't
Roll forward until
We're the disciplined
Habit of our minds"

Compassion
What a great escape
From the tyranny and
Chaos of our time

Compassion
Let it be our
Everyday experience
To be happy and
Free...

To Be
Free

It seems
Our divinely
Belief is but a
Conformity forcing
Us to let go our
Collective freewill

Though the
Belief is good at
The core
It's abused in
His Good Name
As history is
The proof

Come,
Let us put all
Shattered dreams
Together through
Our collective
Awakened spirit
And inspire the
Young...

Human
Divine

We
Alone are
The cause and
Consequence
Of our destiny

We're
The finite
Souls
Holding onto
Freewill

We're
The creators
Of future to be

We're
The masters of
The mighty universe

And yet
We fail to
Reckon the strength
Of the inner being...

It's
Magic

Don't say,
"Its not love
But a brief
Passion"

Don't say,
"We've never
Met before"

Come,
Sweetheart
Let it be known,
"We're in love
From
Births to rebirths"

Let me
Make it perfectly
Clear,
"We've been
The feeling of love
In eternity itself..."

Simple & Plain

Whatever
It may be
Now doesn't
Matter anymore

In the end,
It's the
Pure sleep
That matter
The most

Whatever
Glory
If there is and
Whatever story
To be told is over
In the end

Whatever
We may be
While living, but
We're all equal
In the hands of
The Noble Death,
Essentially...

One Shot Only!

As we're
Born, no sooner
Life silently
Begins with its
Teasing game,
Called,
"Despair and
Death"

Not a friendly
Reality to be
Encountered and
Yet it is waiting
For everyone

As we
Leave this
Realm of chaos
And struggles;
Acknowledging
The beauty of having
A wonderful experience
I mean, once being alive...

Lit
The Spirit

What if
Life means
Happiness,
Why aren't we
Happy today

If freedom
Is the goal of
Our identity
Why aren't we
Rebelling against
The 'Techno-evil"
Today

If we're
The moral
Agents of change
Why aren't we
So docile and
Waiting so long and
For what!

Sleeping
Giants

Without
Morality, human
Just an empty
Shell living for
Nothing

Without
Rational insight
Human is but an
Insignificant flicker
In All That Is

No, no
We don't want
To be measured
While passing through
A well-lited tunnel

Let the
Mind be on fire
And let us be
Triumphant
Against
All odds of life
That is plagued by
Chaos, anxiety and fear...

Beware!

Be aware of
A rigid belief
That can kill
Moral Goodwill

It has, it is and
It shall go on
Impacting the
State of humanity
If silence is the
Answer

Let us
Not forget to
Read the pages
Of the
Bloody history,
Please...

Global
Spark

Damn right,
We've been on a
Wrong track for
Sometime

It's
Been such
A long odyssey
Of struggles;

Failing
To know the
True identity
Up to this point

Is it not
The time to
Understand
The underlying
Meaning of our
Existence in our
Time!

New
Direction

We've been
Going round
And around in
The circles of
No return

Shouldn't
We ask, "Why
Stick around in
Such a merry go
Carousal"

Why not
Jump off the
Crazy ride and
Begin to be an
Awakened
Humans again

Time to
Adapt to new
Reality of the
"Global Village"
Time to be
Friends and not
Strangers while
Soaring to the
Highest realm...

On a
Roller-Skater

Beings
Thrown into the
World of
Constant chaos
And greed of this
"Shinning
Techno- world"

Oh yes,
The super-rich
Taking their dark
Money and hiding,
"Where?" that
We know so well

Why
Don't they
Think of the
Dire societal needs,
So many can live well

All is
Changing quick
And ordinary folks
Keeps falling behind,
In every way to
Catch-up with their
Crazy times...

Turning
Point

We're the
Living perception,
And keep suffering
From the soft feelings
Of alienation, time
After time

Look at
Our collective
Plight today,
The worlds been
Fueled by over
Doses of the
Techno-grip;
Threatening our
Future indeed

In such a
State of anxiety
Why don't we
Reinterpret the
Value of the real
Human again!

Being & Meaning

Being
Always a
Connective link
With everything
In this
Holistic reality
That we've
Come to know

Being is the
Consciousness itself
Through the endless
Social experience

That's where
He grasps his
Own meaning, his
Mission and how to
Fulfill the dream

Being
A continuum of
Moral inspiration
And the greatest
Hope of all that is...

Immortals

What
We had
Is still with us
And will do so
Tomorrow
As well

Nothing
In the world
Dare split
Our two souls

Either
Life or death
Who cares

When we're
The one timeless
Love who should
Never be separated
From our sacred souls...

Swirling Winds

God, eternity,
Creation, good,
Evil and many such
Abstruse issues

All targets of
The human mind
Millennia after
Millennia but no
Success to date

First we tried,
Superstitions but
Didn't work
Later we invented
Geographic Gods
Again we didn't get
The Spiritual Unity,
In return

Well the
Inconclusiveness
Simply got us off the
Right track whence
"Why haven't we
Awakened our souls."

Uneasy

It's
The story
Of our kind,
Yes it's the
Struggle of our
Mental state, all right

The issue is
The uneasy relation
Between
Individual and whole
Throughout the time

We adore our
Individuality for
Freedom, but we
Also want to be
Safe and secured
With the whole as well

That's been
The issue of humanity,
A tough-of-war between
Individual liberty and the
Social cohesion since the
Very beginning...

Inspiration!

Arts,
Poetry and
Humanity all
Come free with no
Rigid impositions,
Either religion or
Whatever else

They're
Mirror of our
Creativity and
Imaginations
In every sense

Arts,
Poetry and
Humanity keeps
Searching,
"Who we're and
How we ought to be"

Arts,
Poetry and
Humanity where
Beauty and truth
Waits always...

Let's
Ride

Come ride
With me to the
Mountain high

Where we can
Gaze the zillions
Stars and be inspired
In this cosmic realm

Come and
Don't wait for
Life is rolling away
Like the swift clouds

Don't wait
Don't hesitate just
Come and let's ride
To the mountain
High where
There is neither
You nor I, but our
Love is the only truth...

Predicament

Crazy
Must be the
Life itself and
Crazy is the
Being without
Understanding
The meaning of
It all

The past was
Half and half and
Future we don't
Know so well
Only
The present
We can shape it
Before it's too late

Not
Materiality
And not the techno
Sophistication, but
The real human is
On trial day by day
For all we know...

Inexcusable

Yesterday
Was a cloudy day
Tomorrow may be
Full of showers and
Storms

And, today
We better keep
The Umbrella ready
That's the way
We've been for
A very long

Today,
We're full of greed
And ready to blow-up
The whole world with
Nukes and many more

Wonder,
"Why aren't we
Ready with the umbrella
Called, "Common sense!"

Once
Upon

Once
Upon folks
Lived simple
And where
Air was clean and
Water so plenty
And the soil so
Fertile

It was a
Agro realm and
Folks worked very
Hard and the family
So happy living under
One roof

Oh yes,
The folks in their time
Were simple and enjoyed
Their bucolic beauty dancing
With fresh air, clean water
And the real organic
Soil...

Epiphany!

Deluxe
Colorful
Edition
Revealing
Modern
Hedonistic
Life style where
Folks living off
Their borrowed
Time

World today
Washed
With greed,
Myopia and
Tribal claims
And sadly,
Where only
Measure is the
Money and
Nothing else

And still folks
Pretending to be
Happy every day ...

Tools of
Survival

On the
Desk, there's
The calendar,
Dictionary, box
Full of blank sheets
All tools to print out
My revolving thoughts,
Indeed

That is how
I begin my early
Morning mental
Gym

That's been
Over sixty
Years of habit of
This ever curious
Mind

That's been
The tools of my
Expressions
And that's been the
Pleasure of my daily
Meditation...

Serendipity

It all began
Between her
And I with a simple,
"Hello" and a friendly
Big smile

Thought
It was just a
Causal greeting,
But we're wrong
From the onset

It took a
While for our
Hearts to reckon,
"It was the beginning,
Already"

Love what
An accidental
Teaser
Love what
A silent fire between
Two strangers...

Take
Note

Time keeps
Slipping away
And the
Memories
Too
Such is the
Ephemeral
Human
Experience
That we face
Between birth
And death only

If so,
Why it takes
Such a long to
Know the value
Of life itself,

Especially
When
We're young,
Healthy and
Very ambitious to
Say the least...

Adaptation

Thinking,
Perceiving and feeling
All shaped by the
Cultural conditioning
Of the mind

It was okay
When the world
Was so big like a
Mega-galaxy

Well we're
Today living
In this "Globally
Shrinking Village"

Its time
To change our
Perception,
Our old belief,
Our false sense of
Superiority and be the
Friends with others...

Confession

I write
The way I feel
Free to express
My inner being

I write
To understand
Deeper meaning
Of the self and the
Cosmic mystique

I write
To meditate
Through my
Time in this
World

I write
Being
Grateful to
The magic of
All there is to
Experience...

Let Live

We live, laugh
And be busy in
Fulfilling our big
Dreams

We call it,
Our Life, our
Existence either
With meaning or
Otherwise

It doesn't
Matter anymore
So long we're
Happy and at peace

Let's
Sing and dance
Today and seize the
Moment on hand,
Carpe diem...

Dear
Heart

**Dear Heart
How long will
You not hear
My heart throbs**

**Dear Heart
Come and make
It up softly for
Times slipping
Away so quickly**

**Dear Heart,
Let's not miss
This chance of
Our youth**

**I say,
"Come and
Make it up
Before it's
Too late to say,
"Gee, we missed
The boat..."**

Depth

Each
A flash of his/her
"Point of view"
Either right
Or wrong, but it's
A pure freedom
Human to be

If the total
Point of
Humanity is on a
Right track,
Unity, liberty and
Happiness shall be
The rewards waiting
In the wing

Each being
An awesome force
That can lift the whole
To the highest peak,
If their point of view
Affirms the real code,
'We're the meaning of
Love, peace and harmony
At all time..

Be
Fearless

Time to
Question
Everything
With good
Intention

Right
Question is
The first shot
From the silos

To hold the
Guardians
In-check from
Their "Double-
Speaks"

Don't be
Timid or shy
Be fearless and
Do exercise
You're right to ask
The right question
At any time and that's
Your freedom indeed...

My Space

It's my
Little office where
On four walls
There hangs the
Pictorial memories
Of my life and time

In the north is
Images of loved
Ones who inspired
Me to go after the
Big dream

In the east,
There is the
Celebrations saluting
My soul mate

In the south is
The display of the
Titles of the books; a
Modest gift to the world

In the west is a
Blank wall where
"Deep Silence" is the
Inspiration sparking
My revolving thoughts...

The
Riddle

Why did we
Forget the
Moral truth or
Objectivity of
Our existence

Why have we
Not fulfilled the
Base ethics to
Refined
Our human
Nature thus far

What have
We done so far
To clarify our
Collective significance
In this turbulent time

Why're we
Still spinning into
This grand sphere of
Self-doubts and debates...

Revelation

World seems
A sinking ship
As forces of
Nationalism,
Terrorism and
Jingoistic fervors
Keep bubbling
So strong

Its happening
When humanity's
In dire need to be,
"One Universal
Agreement
Of the Minds"

Yes to fight the
Global issues of
Our time: nukes,
Climate, cyber hacks
And on-going conflicts
And wars

Let's
Come together
Let's break out of
Th prevailing insanity
Let's learn to save our
Children's dream...

Great
Ride

Let us
Be proud of
Being born as an
Intelligent species

Albeit
We're the
Enlightened
Consciousness
Born to grasp
The moral Self
In this holistic
Reality for sure

Come let's
Be awakened
Spirits, "We're
The ever moving
Force of change for
We're the limitless
Possibilities always..."

Pure Experience

Let's
Come together
And blow off
The Seven sin
Forever from our
Diseased spirits

Yes,
That's the
Only way to reach
The highest peak,
To launch the real
Journey on

If we
Succeed;
That we must
We shall be the
Winners of our
Pure experience,
What is our truth...

Let's
Roll

Gray clouds
Looming over
Our thick heads

Is it not
Time to be
Awakened to
Our
Common sense

Let's not be
Afraid, but face
The challenge
Head-on

Let's
Wake up
And clear-up
The dark clouds
What're looming
Over
Our thick heads...

Magnifique

Oh the
Beauty of
All beauties, so
Close to my heart
And let's fly to the
Heavenly place
Where we shall
Be the truth

Oh the
Dream of all
Dreams
Don't let the
Time slip away

Yes, darling,
This is our time to
Be one united soul
Let it be the
Meaning of our
Genuine human
Experience to the end...

Ascension

Let
Modern
Being
May not be
Deterred

Let his
Determined
Will
Take him to
To the world
Of Peace

Let him
Be
The winner
Don't
Let him go
Off the track,
Ever again...

In Love

Sing softly
My love for the
Night's still young

Be the
True feelings to
Tie our dream
Tonight

Yes,
Darling the
Night's still young
And this is the
Moment to dance
Once again

I say,
"Come and
Let's
Be lost into this
Madness of love"

Yes,
Darling lets
Dance all the way to
Our waiting dream...

Greetings!

Dear
Destiny
Let me
Touch your
Truth

Let me
Tell your of our
Friendship that's
Tailored for
Generations to
Come

Yes, we're
In this celestial
State named,
"L'amoura"

Oh the dream
Of all dreams,
Be my forever in
Love, in love...
In love forever...

Life:
An Ellipsis

What was
True yesterday
Is good for today
What is
Good today shall
Dictate tomorrow

And
There won't
Be any full-stop,
But the world shall
Keep rolling along
The infinite dots

We shall
Always live or
Die in this
Great wheel of
Spinning wheel

Where
Nothing to stop
Our possibilities
That's why life's
An ellipsis all right..

Way
To Truth

Never say,
"Never"
For all shall
Roll toward truth
In the end

Never say,
"Never" as the
World is shaped
By the moral
Courage always

Never say,
"Never" for
Our destiny is
Sealed by the first
Greeting already

Never say,
"Never" for we're
The truth to
Fulfill the meaning,
"Who we're and
What we ought to be."

Fiat lux

Light
What a grand
Inspiration
Atlast to the
Brilliant stars
Where dreams
Are being born

Take me
To the place
Where great
Souls are
Illumining their
Moral insight

Give me
Inspiration,
Give me
Strength to
Make it all the
Way to my truth

Lead me
To the realm
Where I am the
Genuine courage
And freewill always...

Action,
Please

If you care,
I say, take a
Bold stand to
Stop corruptions,
Desperations and the
Senseless destructions

If you care,
Raise your moral
Voice to build a
World of harmony
And hope for all

If you care,
Stop your shallow
Criticisms,
Fake news and go
After the facts

If you care,
To live in the
World you want,
Then stop talking
And start the walk...

Cosmic
Gems

We are
The fascinating
Thoughts, ideas
And point of views
Loaded by the
Cosmic thrills

We are
The brilliance
In this existence
Lifted by the
The great heroes
Of all times

We are
The connection
Between the known
And the unknown
For a meaning

We are
The very
Mystery yet to
Be understand,
Well...

Courage

Mind is the
Window that
Got no limits of
Imagination,
Creativity and
Determination

Yes, it's this
Bold gift of
All gifts remain
In the state of
Contradictions,
Now and then

That is the
Dilemma being
Human born
With so much
Inner strength...

The
Quest

Each to
Grasp the widening
Experience of humanity
Through reason and
Moral insight alone

Let each
Reach out to the
Distant stars to
Turn their dreams
Into reality called,
"Happiness forever"

Let each
Begin to walk the
Walk to the Temple
Of Truth
Where meaning of
The Self to be revealed
For the first time...

Breadth
& Depth

Intelligent
Being seeking
The meaning
Of all-that-is

Indeed,
He's
Sovereign
And born
To be free

Each
An inspiring
Spark of the
World's hope

Let him
Lift humanity
To its deserving
Heights...

Genuine

To act upon
Necessary
Moral
Convictions
Means there
Shall be an
Enlightened
Experience

It's
Time to assess
The validity of
Every avenue
To the Truth

Even
Questioning
The issues of God,
Soul, immortality
And natural evil
Without a fear

No matter
What....in the end,
"We're the
Possibilities, courage
And freewill's."

Dear

Oh yes,
Dear God who's
The inspiration,
But why the world
Still is under the
Shadows of so much
Struggles and pain

God, I mean
The dear Lord,
Oh yes
The sacred object
To fulfill our
Personal selfish
Wants

Let the
Idea of God
Be our
Determined
Will
To change the
World for good

God, oh yes
Our dear Lord
What a craving
Object of zillion
Wants of the
Begging man...

Achilles...

Some says,
"World is
Meaningless,
Other insist,
It's otherwise"

Some says,
"Being is for
Individuality,
Other insist,
Something else"

Young says,
"Let's resolve the
Issues now" and
Old says, "Let's
Ignore 'em all"

Meanwhile
Humanity hangs
On a thin rope of
Hope only and that's
Not good enough...

Dark
Force

Ahh
The issue of
Evil:
Is it an absent
Coherent view
Of reality?

Or is it, simply
Bad choices of the
Misguided beings!

Evil,
Always keep
Increasing the
Value of good

Evil,
What a constant
Struggle of humans
To be free from
It all

Evil,
What a collective
Force of human
Anxiety, fear and
Death...

Boundless

We're
The living
Inspirations and
Million dreams
Yes,
We're the
Cosmic seeds
Of an ultimate
Reality to be
Known

We're
The jewels of
This magnifique
Universe and
We're born
To reveal our
Total truth

Rejoice,
We're the
Boundless and
Infinite possibilities
All the way to the end.

What Reality!

Some people
Think, reality is
A process where
Being is Becoming

Others hold,
Reality is just
A multiple unity
Of all that is

In the end,
Being defines
His reality either
As is or
Something big

Whatever,
It may be,
It all begins with
The illumined spirit
Of every being,
As always...

Open-Mind

Being
Exists to
Know his place,
His understanding
And a meaning while
He's on the trail

Being
What an
Intellectual fire
Power, always
Probing:

"What is
Freedom?
What is truth?
What is guilt?
What is good and
What is not..."

Being,
Indeed a measure
Of his essence,
His action and
The consequence...

Be
Free

We're
Born to share
Knowledge and
Experience in the
Name of harmony
And peace

If faith, rituals
And prayers help,
We go there and
Embrace all that
With open hearts,
If not
We must seek
New ways

Let our
Births be the
Truth-seeking
Adventure and
Not a
Blood spilling
Experience...

Where's Progress

There is
Science,
Philosophy
Metaphysics
And more,
Yet no coherent
Point of view
Thus far

There is
God, wisdom,
Goodwill and
More, yet no
Durable peace
In the world

There are
Eight plus billion
Souls in this
"Info age," but
They're not well
Connected thus far...

Transient

I wonder,
"What if we're
Not real, but fleeting
Souls in a perceptual-
Transition between
Life and death and
Life again"

What if are
Simply the
Adventurers
Of knowledge,
Meaning and
Blind beliefs

What if,
All is one, but
The selfish mind
Thinks otherwise!

Toward
Unknown

**Are still
The prisoners
Caught by our
Subjectivity,
Uncertainty and
Ephemeral opinion**

**Are we still
Conjectural
In judgment of
Our ethics,
Reason and the
Noble mission**

**What if
We are the
Eternal change
And that is the
Only way to
Experience,
"What is our
Only truth!"**

Reflections

In the
Larger picture,
Human indeed
Is a continuum
Truth

In the
Process, he's
The paradigm

Wonder,
Will he
Ever catch-up
With his genuine
Inner being

Will he
Ever realized,
He can triumph
Over the seven sin!

Detoured

Challenge is
How to conduct
Ourselves to live,
Not for us alone,
But for the good of
The whole

Such a simple
Issue not
In the grasp of
The universal
Wisdom yet

Even in our
Modern time,
We've not
Understood,
"What is right?"
"What is just?"
"What is humanity?"
And much more

After thousands
Years, we still
Keep dancing with
One war after another
And ignoring the
Future consequences
To our kids...

Being
Here

To be
Free means,
Having a full
Rational
Understanding
And moral insight

To be
Awakened
Means,
Knowing well
Where you're
Heading for the
Good of all

To be
Happy
Means good
In thoughts,
In words
And in deeds,
Always

To be
Bold means,
You've gain the
Vision of total
Reality, indeed...

The
Force

Being
Contextual,
Defines
The final
Turning point
Of every human
That lived once
And those alive
Today

Wisdom,
That's
The final
Arrival point
Still demands
Disciplined mind

Human
Essence what
A solemn drive
Opening-up all
Possibilities
To make it
Through all...

The
Voyage

**Being,
The only
Image in
The grand
Mirror of
All the
Waiting
Adventures**

**He
Indeed is
The face of
Goodness,
That's why
So majestic in
His ideals and
Dreams**

**Why
He turns into
Midget when
"Implementation"
Knocks his door!**

Crux

The true
Aim is to be
An awakened
Soul and arrive
At a noble
Destination,
Where
Rational and
Morally strong
Folks resides

Time
To take a
Bold stand and
Keep probing
All possibilities
To be part of
Such a
Perfect world

Let us
Learn how
To lift human
Dignity sky-high

And show
We're
Indeed worthy
Citizens of such a
Beautiful realm...

The
Fabric

**All that
Exists
Is reducible
To human
"Consciousness"**

**That's why
Intelligent
Being's worthy
In the
Totality-of-all-
Experience**

**Albeit
Only in such
A milieu
His point of view
Has a meaning...**

Far &
Beyond

Human
What a glorious
Creative spark
Indeed
An exploring
Mind in this
Mighty Universe

Let him
Roll forward
Let him
Probe riddle of
The all riddles and
Never be tired of
His venture...

Search

Certainty
No longer
Valid, today

For we live
In the realm
Of quantum
Thinking
Already

Where
Probality and
Randomness
Defines our
Reality today

Even the
Notions of God
And the Self been
Questioned lately
And don't know

Either
We're evolving
Along a right path
Or simply going
Crazy within
Our 3-lb thinking
Machines or what!

Inscrutable

God,
The first cause,
A posterior necessity
For the conceptuality
Of the human mind
All right

Yet
It leaves petite
Doubt to such an
Assumption,
Time after time
For reason we
Don't understand
That well

Perhaps it's
'Cause many
Millennia
Gone by and
Still we've not
Left the tunnel,
Yet

Also 'cause
Why zealots get
Get away killing
Innocent people
In His name and
Still remain free of
Their guilt's...

Will to
Win

What if
The reality is
Nothing but a
Organic
Complexity

Where
Unity of all
Things exists
At the core

In such a
Unique milieu,
Humans are born
Being imperfect
And keeps chasing
After 'Perfection'
Forever...

Power
Within

Morality
What
Free will in
Action every
Day in every
Way

Morality
Awakens,
"What's we
Ought to be"

Morality,
What a power
Of love, laughter
And dignity of
Every being...

Grand Mirror

We've
Ignited the dark
Passions: violence's,
Wars and never-ending
Tragedies to our kind

That is
What the history
Shows our ugly sins
And our collective
Deeds pages after
Pages and we
Read 'em so
Silently

Let us
Change the
Inner Mirror
Let us refined
Our thoughts and
Actions

Let us
Not forget,
Children shall
See their elders
Faces in the same
Grand mirror one
Day...

Ultimate

Human,
Essentially an
Enlightened
Potential
For he's the
Rational and
Moral force
Of one

Yes, he's a
Conscious
Agent of the
"Moral Will"

Let him
Rise above and
Beyond ignorance
To seek his truth

Let
He drops:
Envy, greed,
Selfishness and
So on and
Let him
Manifest to be
Human-Divine
To the end...

Intrigued

Did we
Know,
We're the
Evolving force
In this continuum
Flow of reality!

Did we
Ever care to
Think,
We're the
Ever glowing
Freewill's

Did we
Ever reckon,
We're the light

We're the
Awareness;
Flying to
New heights
Every sec

Why then
Be ever
Complex and
Doubtful of our
Simple truth!

Janus

Each born
To be an
Awakened soul,
And still an
Ignorant being

Why such
Paradox to
Experience!

Each
An endless
Possibilities
To be free

And still a
Prisoner in
The tribal cage

Why
Such an
Absurdity to
Experience!

In
Chains

When
The world is
Spinning with
Debris from the
Ugly past

The present
Can't escape
The glorious
Blunders and
Myriad sins

How long
Can we keep
Cheating and
How
Long can us
Be in this
Cocoon phase

And not be
The butterflies
To roam the
Universe free...

Insight

My soul,
Yes its
The supreme
Gift of all

What a
Magic to
Go on from
False belief to
The real truth

It's
The very
Essence and
Willing of
My inner being

My soul,
Yes my
Solemn, "Soul"
Guiding me
Toward all that is
Beauty and truth...

Love,
Et Cetera

Once
In love
We thought
It was forever

Well, suddenly
Time changed,
So did our
" Good Feelings"

Today,
Two hearts
Dropping tears in
Two distant places

That's the
Story of two
Hearts thought,
"In love forever"

That's been
The glory of joy
And deep wound;
Thinking, "Being
In love forever..."

The
Game

It's the
Tacit game of
Exerting power
Over others
In a given
Social set-up

Why
Pretend to be
Great
When nothing
Good to offer
In return

Wonder,
Why is it a
Strong desire
To control
Others when
He is a weak
Animal already!

Reckoning

Is it not
Time to awake
The spirits and
Begin the journey
At once

Is it not
Time to rid off
The harmful
Thoughts and
Cheer-up for
A change

Let
There be
New beginning
To seek the
Meaning of
Our worth
Let
There be
Real redemption...

Ethics

So we
Excel to
Think big
Yes,
To live
A life of
Being worthy
Today

But,
Where's
The readiness
Of our collective
Disciplined mindsets

Let's come
Together to
Fulfill the
Children's wishes
And their dreams...

Jewels

Let children
Grow-up with the
Mystical spirits:
To love, laugh and
To live well

Let 'em
Know, "What is
Good is a joy for
All"

"Let their
Inner being seek
Humanity with
Integrity, always"

Let us
Sew right
Fabrics for a
Beautiful world
To be...

Being &
Essence

Opinions
Are ripples
Flowing
Through
The Sea of
Uncertainty

Life too
Is uncertainty
Suspended
Between
Birth to death

Against
Such a reality
Human is boldly
Seeking his meaning...

We, the People

We can
Control
Our opinions
And conduct,
Only

Indeed,
We can
Write the
Script with
Our creativity
And vision
Simply

But, its
The art of
How to handle
The challenges
With calm and
Reason

Well that
Defines our
Significance in
The end...

In Love!

Come on
Babe, let's take
Step one, step two
And three

Let's dance
Cha cha ...all the
Way to the sweet
Night

Come darling,
Let's write the
Lyrics of love and
Fly to the world of
Our dreams

Let's take
Step one, step two
And three darling
To be One forever,
Forever...forever
In eternity

Gauntlet

Folks
If we desire
To live in peace
We need to
Button-up our
Strength, our
Fortitude and
Rational insight

We must
Learn, "How to
Stand up for the
Good of humanity
At every time"

Why do
We wait?
Why not be the
Magnificent beings
To meet the collective
Noble aim while
We got the time!

The
Challenge

What if
We're losing
Our precious
Identity so fast,
Today

Do we care
To correct
The situation
Do we've
The strength to
Demand change
Today

What if
We forgot,
"How to save
The future of
Our kids?"

In that case,
How should
We meet the
Challenge that's
Starring at our
Thick heads!

We
Exists

To be free,
Means to
Cooperate
With all others;
Looking for the
Same

It also
Means,
We must be
Committed to
Our moral
Covenant,
At all time

If not,
There is the
World of
Violence's, wars
And miseries
Only

We
Mustn't
Ignore the
Bloody pages of
The history, in our
Time or any other time...

Boldness

All
Conclusions
Be open to doubt
To clarify the
Meaning of the
Human experience

All
Beliefs
Be subjected to
Moral scrutiny
To measure their
Rational depth

Life
Must be open
To healthy criticism,
To unveiled,
"What is truth?"

Let it be
A stepping-stone
To explore,
"What are the
Possibilities to be
The illumined mind"

Inner
Being

Every single
Being born with
Freedom must
Know well

Freedom
Is valid only,
If there is an
Equal degree of
Responsibility
In return

Yes, that's
The very
Emergence of
Human reality;
Demanding,
Moral judgment
Always

Yes,
To balance
Freedom and
Responsibility to be
The fully-matured
Human being...

Naked
Truth

There is no
Escape from the
Jaws of despair
And death

These are
Two unchanging
Life experience
And that be the
First lesson to
Get smart from
The very beginning

Only the
Spiritual strength
And the rational
Insight would
Free us from the
Situation we're in

Let us be the
Awakened spirits
And learn, "How to
Walk the walk along with
Others seeking the same"

The
Breed

"Who we're"
Let it be
Shaped by our
Highest aim
In life

And not just
Through falsity
And pseudo-claims,
But moral courage
And rational strength

Let it
Reverberate the
Deaf world
Let it
Awaken humanity,
At the very core
Come,
Let us boldly
Meet the truth
Face- to- face...

Being & Morality

In the
Age of
"Information"
There is no
Excuse left, but
To stand-up for
The clarity of
Our collective
Freedom

In the
Age of
"Hedonism and
Greed"
There is not
Much time left
To save our children's
Dream and their future

In the
Age of
"Disorder and
Eroding dignity"
There is no
Time left, but to
Fight for our
Identity and name...

Moral Agents

Truth
In the end,
Shall triumph
Over all the
Conceptual
Premises and
Conclusions

That is
Where the
Power of the
Inner being shall
Surface and carry
Torch of harmony
And hope

That is
When
Truth becomes
A pragmatic reality
And that we must
Know so well...

Bold
Odyssey

I alone
Is my
Bold odyssey,
As I evolve from
Self-consciousness
Toward the eternal
Consciousness

That is
The end point
Where the certainty
Of my true meaning
Begins

Outside of
This solemn
Thought,
All seems
Ephemeral,
Superfluous lacking
Any moral vigor...

Glow
In Night

Drums of
Life keeps
Beating day
And night and

Folks
Keep dancing
Through their
Finite time

Let 'em
Be merry
Let 'em hugs
One another with
Sincere feelings

Soon the
Dawn will crack
And a new day
Will begin with a
Greater meaning
Than yesterday...

Inner
Being

Reality
What a
Flow from
Imperfection to
The perfection

In it all,
Human
What an
Enlightened
Soul to be

Future
What a
Constant
Tease to
Certainty

In it all,
Human
What an
Indomitable
Freewill to be...

Don't
Rush

Hey, hey
Sweet heart,
Don't rush
To the high
Dream so soon

It takes
A while to
Get to the place
You desire to
Reach

I mean,
Not your words,
But sincerity
Is the key to
Open the door

Yes,
Sweet heart
We're talking of
Our future and
Children to be born...

Silent Cry

Soldiers
Returning home
From the battlefield,
But why aren't they
Singing their
Victory Song

Soldiers
Passing through
The war torn zones
And hiding their deep
Feelings of shame

What a
Heart-braking
Scene,
Mothers tossing
Away their babies
In the air

And
Brave soldiers
Catching 'em
With hurtfulness
What a saddest
Human tragedy to
Witness, once again...

142

Confucian Goal

Wiseman
Directed to
Cultivate:
Yi, li and ren
To become
Chun-tzu,
Meaning to be a
Superior being

Those who
Valued his wisdom,
Brought peace to
The world and
Those didn't
Wrote the history
Full of bloodstains

Yi, li and ren
All for the human
Perfection, but
Sadly the world
Failed to practice
Such an ethical
Dream...

143

The
Way

Tao means
To be in harmony
With the mighty
Universe

Tao is
To be in harmony
With the fellow
Human beings

Tao
Affirms,
W*uwei* which
Is to effortlessly
Deal with all that is

Tao holds
The cosmic void
From which all
Things evolve and
To which they return...

The Passage

It all begun
In a random
Quantum state
Which was but
"Nothing"

No sooner
Inflation took
Its course and
Everything's been
Changing ever
Since
Matter, dark
Matter and dark
Energy kept dancing
Through timelessness

Here we're
Today still "bobbing"
Into the anticipated
Demise of the Universe...

Discovery

While being
Alive
Let us be the
Breath-taking
Discovery of
Our selves

And indeed
Let i be the
Paradigm shift
In our time

Yes,
Let it be the
Moral awakening
To save our dignity
And freedom for sure...

Mighty Gift

Always
Thinking,
Wondering
Even imaging
This magic called,
"What is being
Human?"

Is he a
Celestial seed
To give meaning
To all that is

Is he a
Cosmic force
To change the
World for good!

Human
Always an
Enigma, but
Still a real deal
Who is a shining
Gift of freewill...

Great Thrust

Being
Alone is the
Innate force of
Good

Let him
Evolve from
The core to the
Needy world
At-large

Moral
Action that is
What the world
Must get ready
To go with full
Confidence and
Courage today...

Be
Smart

Every
Poor kid,
Keep running
'Til there's
A place they're
Welcomed with
Open arms

Let 'em
Explore 'til
They've found
Their own meaning
In this world washed
With chaos and
Greed

Let 'em
Keep rolling
Till they begin to
Lift others like
They were once...

Pure Thought

Brahman,
What a
Pure thought
With no-string
Attached

Brahman
Is All There Is
And nothing to
Claim, but the
Elegant Truth
It's called,
"Tolerance and
Understanding"

Brahman
Got no name, but
The holistic reality
Of all that is here
And beyond

Brahman,
An intelligent
Essence of our
Consciousness
With no tribal
Claims imposed ...

As Is

In this
Crazy changing
World of blunders
And sins

Being is
Seeking his
Center point
With ethics and
Courage at every
Single struggling
Turning point

In such
A swirling fate
Let his inner
Courage keep
Rolling toward
The set noble goal...

To Be

Awareness,
Yes awareness
Shall free us from
The imposed false
Narratives and
Skewed beliefs

We humans
Are the
Transforming
Moral agents
And must
Take charge

Let us
Look beyond
The divided
Mind-sets and
Begin to
Understand,
"We're the
Gifts of only ONE
Who may carry
Different names...